The Hiding Place

*to the memory of
my mother and father
and their generation*

THE HIDING PLACE

Tom Duddy

ARLEN
HOUSE

The Hiding Place

is published in 2011 by
ARLEN HOUSE
an imprint of Arlen Publications Ltd
42 Grange Abbey Road
Baldoyle
Dublin 13
Ireland
Phone/Fax: 353 86 8207617
Email: arlenhouse@gmail.com

Distributed internationally by
SYRACUSE UNIVERSITY PRESS
621 Skytop Road, Suite 110
Syracuse, NY 13244–5290
Phone: 315–443–5534/Fax: 315–443–5545
Email: supress@syr.edu

ISBN 978–1–85132–013–4, paperback

© Tom Duddy, 2011

The moral rights of the author have been asserted

Typesetting ¦ Arlen House
Printing ¦ Brunswick Press

Contents

9	The Touch
10	Local History
11	Small Holdings
12	Barns
13	In that country
14	The Language of Visitors
15	Racing Festival
16	Havoc
17	Locals
18	Nearest Neighbours
19	Left Bank
20	Rest
21	The Shallows
22	Talker's Country
23	Out of the Rain
24	Their Child
25	The Disappointment of Toys
26	The Book of Names
27	Side Street
28	Woman Trying to Do Everything
29	The Quiet Life
30	High Grass
31	The Art of Visiting: Past Masters
32	The Street Collector
33	Far Cry
34	The Hard Earners
35	Brothers and Sisters
36	The Café
38	The Discovery
39	Public House
40	Picture
41	The Delivery Man

42	Folk Museum
43	The Elderberry Tree
44	Remains
45	The Life of Robert Frost
46	The Problem of Memory
47	Good Casual Jacket
48	The Origin of Table Manners
49	The Small Hours
50	Two Poets
51	The Fear of School
52	New Complete Geography
53	The Holiday
54	Garden Party
55	The State of Nature
56	The Hiding Place
57	The Framing Shop
58	The Rights of Man
59	Three Recurring Dreams
60	Doorways
61	Table for One
62	Convalescent, with Blue Deck Chair
63	The Good Host
64	About the Author
64	Acknowledgements

The Hiding Place

The Touch

If a child fell from a tree, or raved
with fever, or a father came in hurt
from the fields, I was the one who raced
down the roads to the far side of the town,
to the house by the river, glad
of the chance to pass one more time
through the high clanking gates
into the avenue that would slow me

to a crunching walk under the dark,
cher-cherking, rook-swaying canopy.
It never took more than the one
rat-a-tat-tat to bring to the door
the doctor's wife whose briskly gentle hands
once fixed my collar as I stood in the rain.

Local History

The men there, then, were most at peace
when they clashed with the land itself,
making light of the cut and thrust
of the thistle in the cornsheaf.

The women worked harder still, closer
to the breath of animals, further
removed with each passing year
from their first dream of largesse.

*Their farms have been swept clean
into one far-reaching field, like
a great clarifying idea inferred
from a muddle of small dark thoughts.*

The man who bulked large against
the sun as he pranced at the top
of the harvest cart, fetching sheaves
off the prongs of forks flying up

from below, is dead, his house rented
to a young commuter 'who keeps
himself to himself, as he's entitled.'
The woman who was famous

for her hearty management of dogs,
pigs, calves, and roaming flocks of birds
is dead, her house for a time a barn,
now itself disused, grass up to the sills.

Small Holdings

When I go back there now I no longer ask
how anyone is, who has died, or who's home
from the States; or if there's word of the nephew
who went to work against all tradition
in the flower factories of Holland.
Today I sit as calmly as they do, the embers
ticking over deathless in the yellow ash;
and I turn my eyes to the streaming window,
as they do, only when their neighbour goes by,
high-stepping his way through the wet grass.
Especially I do not ask how he is.

Our eyes return all at once to the world
of colour by Technicolour where Jerry
has caused Tom to run full tilt – WHAM! –
into an anvil, and Tom has slid, table-shaped,
to the ground, only to repair to the chase,
not a mark on him in the next scenario.

Barns

High in the gable of the concrete barns
(built in the 30s by uncles, one of whom
vanished in London when I was four)
the netted window still lets in the birds.

Under the hushing roof, the mortar hives
of the swallows still encrust the rafters.
And still nailed high by the doors (those
loud old metalworks) is the tool-box

from which I once drew out, tasselled with webs,
the first real book I ever read, *The Thirsty Land* –
cover of sunset-greens, a rifleman
on the horizon turning in his saddle

to view the great skull of a steer,
the last chapters missing,
leaving the main character, an Easterner,
flailing in a burning barn, forever

trying to free the screaming horses.

In That Country

news of a death still brings out a grieving militia
armed to the teeth with a murmur and a gesture.
Limping, livid-jawed, wild-haired, skewed
at the hips, bulky in their coats, breathless, they
descend on death. Cavalierly, they troop between
the chief mourners and death. Pausing, mouthing,
grasping, they leave everything unsaid, as if
a full-spoken word must be the coin of death. Outside,
their mourning done, they find their voices again,

praising the dead cheerfully now, as if the whole truth
had suddenly become the invention and patent of death.
After the slow journey to the chapel, after the one
Sorrowful Mystery, they disband, drifting back
to where they came from, never minding what it is
death comes for, their one and only life.

The Language of Visitors

When visitors from abroad (including those
who know the country well) say such things as:
The calves were found in the vegetable garden
or *We had lunch with the family at one*
or *The children were sent to their rooms,*
there is always something not quite right
about their observations. Is it the exactitude –
the nicety of each full sentence – that snags?
Or the polite perception of each event?
Or the presumption of urbane community?

In reality, that garden would have had
a red-shanked jungle of rhubarb growing wild
down the middle of it, all the corners
no-go areas of nettles and drenching grass.
Lunch would have been a heavy meal, quickly downed.
And the sending of the children to their rooms
would have been a sudden U-turn of mood,
a change of face, a father roaring like mad,
his children running dazed in the farmyard.

Racing Festival

The reason I come here is not the horses
(a rumble and outcry on the horizon)
but these carnival odours of plastic
and bruised grass; and the hawkers' bric-a-brac

of water rifles, tea-sets, cap-guns, dolls,
foot-pumps, and hammers with slender handles;
and the Wheel of Fortune and other tricky sports
with rings, cards, darts, and tickets rolled in straws.

Here nothing is guaranteed; there is no value
for money; the hammer may snap in two
at the first attempt to crack a hazelnut
on the hearthstone; and the gauge will soon twist

off the blue foot-pump. The youngest kids
no longer know what the hell a cap-gun is
and wouldn't be seen dead in hard little stetsons;
the Wheel of Fortune man is impersonal

and sullen, wiping the coins off his reds
and blacks, as if they were his by rights.
Here among cheap-jacks and trick-o-the-loopers,
among these winners poorer than losers,

I am elated, light-hearted, beside myself.

Havoc

All our lives we longed for storms,
longed to see the covers whipping
off the supine country,
the boundary trees suddenly
dishevelled and uproarious,
the long grass pressed blue and vivid,
paling towards infinity.

When the storms were over,
they might leave in their wake
a spreadeagled oat stook,
perhaps a disbound sheaf,
a clean-snapped alder branch, an inkling
of washed-out light over the trees,
straws on the road near the town.

LOCALS

The glass of Jameson is the only thing here
that holds the light, drawing all eyes shyly
towards it, as towards a sanctuary lamp.
Only when you retreat to the window where

the sun has been long trapped, battened, and dimmed
in the glazing, and you have sipped and swallowed
your first mouthful, do the men at the bar resume
their telling of a murmured underhand story.

Nearest Neighbours

In our house no animals dare cross the threshold
but here dogs lie everywhere – there are two
curled near the ashes, another under the table.
This one suddenly swings back its head to bite
and avidly snuffle the flaxen inside of its leg.
One of the women brings a piece of cake
on a wide knife and slides it into my cupped hands
while she goes on talking to someone by the fire.

But halfway through I am chased out to play
with the other children; and they (and therefore I)
collect fistfuls of sand from a dune at the door
and race to a derelict enclosure of straw-gold,
desiccated dung-hills into which we throw
as far as we can the fistfuls of sand, and then
race back to the dune for more. Blitz after blitz
does not bring out the bees. *There are no bees,*

I think, as my hand grows a glove of wet sand.
When it's time to go I don't know where I am.
I cannot see our house or the trees around it.
The children laugh and show me which dark field
to cross. Even when I am out of their sight
I do not run, not even under cover of the trees.
When I reach our house no one says a word,
not even to ask what kept me so long, as if
they are the ones who have explaining to do.

Left Bank

This old street, which still dreams of being
central again one day, cannot change itself.
The new shops are always the same kinds
of shops – small places exhaling exotica,
wholly dark inside, their windows filled
with icons, bangles, guides to Zen,
and small decorated tin boxes. New cafes, too,
but all, like those that went before,
serving breakfast all day long. The people

who come down this far don't need much
but they need to sit, sometimes for hours,
leaning into each other, the better to talk
and talk. Even those who sit alone
will sometimes smile or shake their heads,
their lips moving now grimly, now sweetly.

Rest

I drifted off for no longer, I am sure,
than half an hour or so, but I wake
to find the fire out, the room dark,
a shiver at my back, the light still on

in the dining room but no one there,
a hum of voices coming from somewhere
in the house – no, coming from a place
further off than the house can contain.

They're giving me time to heal,
but I can hardly wait for all life
to return, for the power to rise,
totter, toddle, shuffle, waltz, race

to where the warm and wicked laughter is.

The Shallows

High summer. The stench of sea-weed
in the hard-cured streets, the water
in the river so low the river-bed
is an archipelago of ooze and mud islands.
Strangely uninteresting; not even the glint

of a pram hood or bicycle wheel
to catch and then appal the eye.
Where now is the deep, voluminous river
of winter, spring, and early summer?
The red corrugated sheds stand clear

and distinct at last, no longer foil
to their own reflections. Likewise the trees
that weep in the yards that come down
to the edge of the riverbank, the houses
behind them right way up for once

under a downturned sky.

Talker's Country

If you know things that they do not, keep them
to yourself, and lose yourself as soon as you can
in the give-and-take of grim prediction.
If a local tale is told in which one man

stands out as worse than all his neighbours,
don't be the first to wonder aloud if
some injustice has been done. If someone else
is framed for the sake of one wicked laugh,

then laugh you must as well, if you want to uphold
the night and keep the gathering going.
What matters here is not the facts as such,
not even the one sad fact that must bring

a timely dark relief when all gazes waver
and bend to the floor, and laughter comes to grief.
As soon as that moment comes, someone will tell
the tale of the dead man's father and the midwife,

or the tale of his father's father in the days
before running water; and then all eyes
will be raised up again, more dazzled than before,
everyone laughing till he cries.

Out of the Rain

Bizarre premises! Just look at what's here –
sad ceramic bears in suits and frocks, some
supporting brollies, others leaning into prams!
And life-size ducks and geese, cast in coldest glaze,
all wearing hats and scarves! Underneath all these,
reduced to 12.99, are little whole families
of cut-glass animals the sizes of bees,
rotating on silver trays. Bizarrest of all –
glued to fat fiddles, flutes and concertinas –
are the porcelain peasants, each one with a face
like the print of a bleeding thumb, all of them
seated in chairs that are backed as high as thrones.
This is no small place, and there's another level

with more cabinets full of figures so smooth
and cold they can hardly stand for creatures.
There are three assistants, each with a counter
and cash-register, each dressed like an air hostess,
each beautified to within an inch of her life.
More patient than any is the man whose presence
is a complete surprise – you come round the corner
of the glass case that dazzles with china fauna
and there he is, solemn, transfixed, impassive,
primed to act if you should dare to pocket
a crystal cat or porcelain fiddler. His gaze
must follow you to the door beyond which
there rages the passing life of the street.

Their Child

It takes me half a second too long
to get their names out, though I knew
who they were the moment they stepped
out of the crowd, hailing me cheerfully.
I stand amazed, trapped and amazed
in the motionless city-centre heat.
There are questions I cannot ask.

Or be asked. Too much and too little
has happened since the wedding day,
when I last stood in their company.
I call out the names of people not seen
or heard of since that day. (About one
in particular I betray a sudden desire
to hear some word, but there's none.)

Their giddy child ignores my bright hello
and goes on looking daggers through me.
She leans and tugs, made bolder by
their gentle pleas to stop, and now
she is leading them away from me.
There's just time for one last quick wave
before they are lost again in the crowd.

The Disappointment of Toys

In the bigger bedroom where a fire was lit
on this one evening every year, we played
with all our might, punishing the bright red
two-note concertina, the hard-cheeked doll

whose eyes stared dead ahead or clicked shut
according as she was tilted up or back,
the little yellow van that enclosed so strangely
behind tiny windscreens a real portion of dark.

Near to tears at first, we hummed and revved
and spoke in tongues, so that whoever looked in
at the door would not suspect a thing, would see
only children lost in play, and the good fire.

The Book of Names

Each time that a child was due
we bent over a book of names
for boys and girls. Over all
the familiar ones (the names
of the loved and unloved alike)
we shook our heads.
In the end we took
from a saga names that meant
the proud one, the light one –

no one we ever knew.

SIDE STREET

I don't often pass through this part of the city,
though it's on my way uptown as the crow flies.
I don't feel at home here, or streetwise – it's cold,
even when the sun is warming the chimneys,

and dark to boot. My footsteps lose their beat,
the paths are so skewed, so irregular here.
The people are not the same as mainstreet people –
a woman comes dashing out of the shoe repair

(Heels-While-U-Wait) shop and cries *Sorry*; pieces
of burnt paper float from somewhere behind me,
and the man loping rapidly ahead of me
without looking back shouts *Shag off, will ye!*

(but not angrily) at some guys just out of range
of the corner of my eye. They say nothing at all,
these guys, as the loper increases his lead,
nor do they overtake me. The hot sharp smell

of burnt paper darts to the back of my throat,
and I think a small fragment, like a green flake
of distemper from the wall of an old porch,
has landed on my shoulder, but I can't check

or be seen to brush it off. Stepping into mainstreet
is like returning through the looking-glass without
a moment's notice – shoppers tucked in behind me,
not a thing on my shoulder, slight catch in my throat.

Woman Trying to Do Everything

The engulging bulk of the leaf-
and-litter scattering wind
stalls her for a moment in mid-step
as she wheels the sleeping child
through the automatic doors. She

manages to keep a loaded hold-all
in precarious position
on the back of the pushchair
while edging the whole ensemble
forward, at the same time

pressing a phone against her hair,
trying to hear, trying to get
clarity, trying to make herself
heard over the commotion of the street.
And still she has not neglected to let

her hips and thighs – shaped to best effect
in crackling denim – do whatever it is
they have to do, even on a day
such as this, as the cold rain
starts to drop heavily again.

The Quiet Life

Here they dread the sun like they dread
the ashen-faced newsbringer. The sun
disturbs; summer is a burden, hardly
bearable, the air tense with equal measures
of promise and foreboding, the hedgerows
ticking and bristling with excess of life.
They are most at home here in grey winter
clothing, feeling half-hidden as they peer
out from under clenched brows, their eyes
half-closed against whatever light there is.

They are nearest to being happy here in churches
where they may rest in the public dark, listening
to the rise and fall of echoes in the chancel,
unable to hear one clear thing being said
before going back out to the world, unchanged.

High Grass

This time last year we joked about the state
of her front gates, while she, down on one knee,
chucked drooling brushfuls of Brilliant White
into flaking weals of rust.
                        We were ironic, too,
about signs of summer in this neck of the woods –
the wrappers and cans as bright as mushrooms
across the newly mowed green; the back wall
of the community centre running red again
with young love's equations; and OF COURSE
the thrill of lying awake all night again to hear
the best of Chopin from the ghetto blasters!

A sudden sobering of mood then as she left
the paint brush across the tin, straightened (stiffly,
in stages, like a weight-lifter), and came to stand
before me, pulling herself together, pressing
her gold-rims up and back before laying a hand
on the wall between our lives.
                              Your children,
she said, have grown SO tall, SO tall. Do you EVER
feel the time! And both of us stood in awe then
for a moment, prayerfully shaking our heads,
as if to misdirect a god, divert some evil eye.

This summer her own tall sons go in and out,
hardly seeing us, hardly speaking. The scrolls
of iron weep with rust, the high grass leans
everywhichway in the garden, and the sycamore –
which the boys SWORE they'd trim back last winter –
scrapes its leaves against an upstairs window where
the curtains have stayed drawn since early in June.

The Art of Visiting: Past Masters

Even as they were still coming in
through the porch, they were already
shouting out jokey slanders, thus
giving the household no choice
but to welcome them heartily in.
We children loved the new order
of loud good cheer, and learned to tell
the difference between stories meant
for us and stories meant to send us
away to play. (We learned, too, that fathers
and mothers had in them a laughter
to which children were not equal).

If we fell asleep where we played,
we would be woken by the pushing back
of a chair, by the shearing draught
from an open door, by the clangour
of fire-irons as some lost time
was made up for with great vigour.
After the departure, it took awhile
for mothers and fathers to remember
the voice in which they were able to say
that it was late now, and time for bed.

The Street Collector

It was so good to be out
on the frantic streets again,
that I did not lose courage

until deep in the afternoon
when I began to baulk
at the thresholds of the heat-

hawing doorways, and to get
in the way of those taking short
cuts through the spaces

I was stepping out of or into. Once,
I found myself at a standstill
beside a collapsible table

behind which there stood the only full
beaming person I'd seen all day.
Before I had time to wonder

if his smile was the smile
of the fraudulent collector
they've been tracking all summer

on the radio phone-ins, I had scooped
from the chaff in my pocket
a handful of coins, all silver

and gold, and poured them in the tilted
bucket, feeling only faintly like
a wrong-footed greenhorn.

FAR CRY

Once, when a voluminous wind snatched at one
of our American balloons and whupped it
up and away from us, we set out – some
of us crying – across the shelterless width

of a neighbour's field. We tried to run faster
than we'd ever done before, but were kept
to a high-stepping dream-struggle by cushions
of moss-thickened grass that our boots went

sinking through. At a gap in the horizon wall
we were trapped in the hoof-gouged, puddled
earth where fragments of sky lay mirrored
at our mud-locked feet, until we mustered

the will to lurch, half-lurch and lurch again
on to solid ground on the other side.
From there we could see a church spire, the roofs
and chimneys of a town, a small pinewood

and a playing field, all pressed in together
like a kingdom in an illustrated story, though
the ground itself on which we stood had in it
nothing except crooked little floors of stone

and a crop of dead white stalks. When we plunged back
through the gap, it took us a while to see the house
that was ours, as if we had travelled further
than we thought, and by a different route.

The Hard Earners

They killed time in a daze
in the sniffling schoolroom
until they were free at last

to learn the hard way how
to inure their hands to earthwork,
stonework, mortarwork; how

to take to heart the absolutes
of measure, rule and mark; how
to send a handsaw yapping

straight down a pencilled line.

Brothers and Sisters

The fellows who travelled the farthest,
trudging in from the poorest townlands,
were the bravest and most obdurate of all.
They would not read, except sullenly, word
by hard-earned word; they would not spell,
except nerve-rackingly, letter by half-guessed
letter; they would not learn off verses, let alone
recite them in the sing-song way; they would not
nicely pronounce any word in which
their fathers' accents were disowned.
They brought upon themselves spectacular wrath.

They were struck, whole-handedly, across the face,
first on one side, then the other; they were cuffed,
suddenly and sharply, on the back of the head;
they had the sally rod made to slash and burn
across the fingers of both hands, which they barely
    nursed
on their way back to their desks, their eyes barely
    watering.
In the schoolyard they ran by themselves, ghosting
in and out of the trees that were out of bounds.

When the school day ended, they were the first
to the door. When their time was done, they were the
    first
to leave the parish, making for London, Manchester,
    or the US
where they always already had brothers and sisters.

The Café

The best time here is this
heavenly lull between
elevenses and lunch hour
when I have all to myself
for company the waitress
who cannot stop finessing,
finessing. She repositions
a menu card; she pushes in
a chair; she reassembles
the cruets back into sets
that click smartly together;
she wakes up the flowers
of the day and makes them
stand taller in their vases.
(Only once has she spoken
half-personally to me, though
I didn't catch what she said.
It was the time a hail shower
cascaded out of a violet sky
darkening rapidly over the gables
of Shantalla, blew fiercely
across the car-parks, and whacked in
the doors, scattering the menu cards).

Though I always ask for one
coffee – regular, black – she
never presumes to guess.
And so each day is a new day.
Which is as it should be.
There is an understanding
that there is no understanding.
This way it remains a mystery
where one has to go when
one rises up, brow furrowed,

urgently checking the time
as one heads for the cash-desk.
There is some joy – more than
she can know – in dropping
the generous tip, nodding
and smiling and turning
clean away before the coin
stops spinning in the wine-glass.

The Discovery

Under the sliding layers of letters
(mostly US airmails) that filled
the scented sideboard drawer I found
a small, red-ribbon-bound white box.

I only half-understood that day
why she came into the room
so swiftly and without a word
and did what she did so firmly,

as if she must never need to do
such a thing again. Even
as I raised the lid, she took the box
from my hands and thrust it back

among the letters; she pushed the drawer in
jerkily at first, then suddenly
so abruptly that the clink-clank
of the handles was rapid and shrill.

She guided me from the room, still
without a word, down through the house,
out through the porch, into the street where
the other children were playing till dark.

Public House

We're laughing already at the thought of someone
whose accent and mindset we have to a T.
And this is how the night will pass, since no-one
will have the heart to say how they are, exactly.

What I'm feeling tonight is not grief, exactly,
(since all those close to me are alive and well),
yet a feeling like grief is earthing me to the floor
in the darkness beneath the rollicking table.

PICTURE

Here is one I tried to take
in the era before flash-bulbs
of the inside of the house (now
a ruin) in which I was born.
I pointed the Kodak into the dark
upper pane of the kitchen window
in the hope that it might record
more than the living eye could see.

But no matter how I tilt it
there remains my own image,
camera to eye, blocking out, I imagine,
some moment lost forever

in the next layer of chemicals –
my brother by the radio, my sister
by the table of basins and cans,
my father framed in the light
of the backdoor like the departing figure
in Velázquez's *Las Meninas*.

The Delivery Man

When the delivery man called after tea
he let in before him such an easterly,
and he stepped down the hallway so briskly,

and he smiled so flushingly, yet so briefly
and with so little knowledge of us,
and with such freedom from all accretion,

and with such innocence of all connection,
that our spirits flickered to life at once,
saltatorially. We cleared our throats

in greeting, and before we knew where we were
we had reached consensus on the lengthening
of the days, now that spring was here.

Such rustling, such quick society, such self-
forgetting! In his eyes, we were still citizens
of the world, with everything still to play for.

But then, while the smiles were still breaking
on our faces, he was gone. The house closed in fast
behind him and grew warm again, and airless
and secure. And dreaming once more overcame us.

Folk Museum

On your right, after you take your ticket,
you'll see a glass case of guns – one old pistol
outshining all the rest – laid out under
the tunic of a soldier who was wounded
during our Civil War, the bullet-hole
neatly preserved above the pressed pocket.

There's a table of radios and clothes irons
(the things most in need of a good dusting here),
and then a wall-cabinet, looking newly installed,
of rows of fishing lures that don't look that old,
or old enough to be here. Under a layer
of reflective glass lie the coins, the coins

that should remind one of something – some scene
at a fair or stall – but nothing comes. Outside,
the backyard is a revelation, not just because
of the burgeoning sun but because of the ploughs,
carts, and harrows lying at all angles, dropleted
and gleaming in the aftermath of recent rain.

There's more colour than you'd expect – the
   cartwheel's
chalky pink, the green of a maker's name embossed
on the handle of a plough, the blue of the one
stone roller. Go to the far side, now, with the sun
at your back, and see how the grass, having closed
over the rutted wheels, is halfway to the axle-trees.

The Elderberry Tree

I

Because it was the first fine day of spring
(a mêlée of gulls over the playing fields,
the roads of the estate suddenly bone dry),
I drove to the country to see my father.

But it was a weekday, a working day,
and he was not prepared for visitors.
I went out into the fields, the wild fields
where he has not gone for years. But the fields

were not prepared for me either; they kept
their distance, and were cold in spite of the sun.
Worst of all, the storms of January
had uprooted and cracked the elderberry tree,

the elderberry tree that once stood in the fourth corner
of the world. I walked and walked, but the fields
kept their distance, and I was alarmed
by curious cattle that massed behind me.

II

Later, moving off, waving out, I saw
that I had trespassed, had stumbled on the future.

Remains

The man diminished to a tribal fetish
far down in his coffin of American oak
was all his life so distant and friendless
that even the soundest villagers here
are at a loss for words of praise, and fail
to murmur the customary absolutions.

Some of these mourners I have not seen
for a quarter of a century or more.
The years are flying. You're looking well,
Long time no see – this is all we have to say
on finding ghosts of children still visible
behind crimson jowl and bristling sideburn.

The sudden return, too, of the repressed!
Someone I had completely forgotten
is striding towards the exit door,
his hands slung together in a gesture
of manly respect for the dead, on his face
the same wry smirk he had in the school-yard.

As we file from the funeral parlour, (slowly,
though the heavens are opening), I find myself
hanging back, waiting for the coast to clear.

The Life of Robert Frost

The place at which I keep the marker
in my condensed edition of the life
is the last page of the early years
in which the forty-year-old poet,

not long before the voyage back
to New England, grows dejected
and wonders if he's lost the gift,
if gift indeed he ever had.

He can't foresee a summer's night
in Vermont, seven years on
in 1922, when he'll work
through the small hours till dawn,

stop for awhile to marvel at
himself and the first light, return
to the table and begin to write
the first words of a perfect poem.

As I switch from the page of doubt
to the page of triumph, back and forth,
like some child with a holographic toy,
I seem compelled to hold the poet

in England, full of doubt, and tilt him
forward to that summer's night
just long enough for me to glimpse
the way a future shimmers there.

The Problem of Memory

I

This evening as I crossed Quincentennial Bridge
there were traces of earth, dark earth, on the road,
fallen perhaps from a truck delivering topsoil
to a new suburban garden. Instantly

II

I am walking past a barn that stands as high
and tilted as a church against the sliding sky.
My mother lives again in the light that I carry,
pensive as she steps through the forests
of groundsel. I carry the light she's alive in
the light that gutters in the smoking globe,
that gutters to the flat blue

point of extinction before it straightens
to a flourish of wall-climbing shadows.

III

Nothing of that time or place remains.
Death and history have passed through them,
I-now a distant relation of me-then.
There are only these images, too familiar
for imaginings, too orderly for dreams.

Good Casual Jacket

The good casual jacket does not go inside
the wardrobe but hangs from one of its doors.
The wardrobe exudes dresses, shirts, suits, none kept
for old time's sake – that's not like us – but kept.
Nothing here is like us; these are the props
of our public lives, this room the backstage
in which the worst may come to the worst.

Between us, we can still put on a show.
We are at our best now, not at weddings
(where she still dances, and I still shed the tears)
nor at christenings (where we both grow cold
praising hats and children), nor at burials
(where we're still the most uneasy mourners)
but here on the housing estate, come summer,

when she puts on her good casual jacket,
and I my lightest raincoat, and we walk out
together, and the children of the estate
are reassured by the measure of our
leisurely step, and their fathers and mothers
are reassured by our conversation, of which
they can only hear the sound, the murmur.

The Origin of Table Manners

Foiled by magic, I close my Lévi-Strauss.
I cannot apply myself anymore now
to the origin myths of the Arapahoe,
Hidatsa, or Sioux. These tales (of the toad-girl
and the sun's canoe; of the stone boy
and the moon's husband; of the porcupine,
master of coldness; of the grebe, master of thaw
and rewarming; of the sun caught in a snare;
of the origin of dogs, daylight, and islands)
are harder to follow than anything
in our handbooks of modern physics.

I cannot *picture* the sun and the moon
travelling together in the same canoe,
or take in all the detail on Kadaua
and the origins of night: Too many
marvellous turns of events, too many
permutations of human, beast, and star,
too many changes of heart in midriver.

The Origin of Table Manners is the English title of a work
by anthropologist, Claude Lévi-Strauss

The Small Hours

A siren far out on the public road
breaks the circle of acid thought, and I turn
to find her pressed close, warm and palpable.

As I shape myself under and around her,
I listen for her breathing, so even and slow,
the pauses so long-drawn-out that each new

intake is like a last-moment revival.
As thought gives way to love, the rhythm falters,
her breathing lurches and comes fitfully,

a name, hardly a name, is drily mouthed,
and I enclose her hand all-roundly
and hold it, hold it, while the dream rages.

Two Poets

In Galway they either took a taxi or got a lift north along the lovely Connemara coast to Cleggan ...
– Anne Stevenson, *Bitter Fame: A Life of Sylvia Plath*

When the two inseparable poets passed
through the city where I'm living now,
they passed within twenty miles of the village
where I was living then, their distance
from my world absolute. How much of the city
did they take with them that September day
into a future that was raging towards them
faster than they could know? As they came out
of the railway station, did they hear the outcry
and commotion of the animals in the slaughter-
house that used to stand down the road
from the Patrician Boys' Band House?
Before they climbed into the car for the island
did they catch at the edge of their visual field
flashes of the livid, cacophonous gulls
                that circle to this day
in the sky over the hospital?

The Fear of School

Dependent on all, independent
of each, the good conversation
has become a thing in itself,
wheeling from one to another,

each of us keeping it going
with the touch of a pun or story –
even middling ones, old ones,
bad ones will do, so good

is the evening, the fellow-feeling,
the encouraging wine. And yet,
just there, just now, when there was
a slowing down, a falling back

down and inward, a straying
of all eyes to the window
on to the darkening garden,
I saw again, as clear as ever,

a room, a boarded ceiling
(on which for years I counted
countless prayers, full of fear),
a mirror, a fender, a painted hearth.

New Complete Geography

How far the species has come, now that at last
the *New Complete Geography* – having dealt with
weather and climate, soil, sea, and rainfall,
population and the growth of cities –
concludes with a section on our unjust world.

After the heart-warming cartoon graphics
showing the ten categories of cloud;
after the neat depictions of meanders
and folded mountains; after the sketches
of an early nucleated settlement;
after the colour pic of an olive grove;
after the focus on Benidorm; after
the woodcut of the bristling soldiers
of Cromwell's army on a river bank; after
the photograph of caribou in Canada
come the bar charts for our unjust world.

The conscience of the world-spirit pricks itself
and the figures of privation become grist
to the mill of our most promising children.
Nothing remains to conquer now in either
the order of nature or the order of grace.

The Holiday

Once, for a week, we stayed
in a Georgian house belonging
to old friends in Dublin:
Three storeys, plus basement,

tall impractical windows,
high impractical ceilings,
oceans of light in the long gardens,
the hall's echo hushed in the rooms.

The hump on my back
felt like bound wings
beginning to loosen and flex,
and I spent the first few days

going in and out of the rooms,
up and down the wide stairs,
breasting the ample space,
light-hearted, learning to fly.

Garden Party

At some strange distance, the good children
are playing among the metal chairs
in the patio; laugh after laugh
goes up from a group that still loiters
by the dead barbecue; old old friends
look well pleased to assemble again
on awkward ground under the sycamore;
the evening sun leaves all impressions

at the edge of consciousness; and an air
of lateness shimmies in the trees.
I almost reach across the table
towards the woman opposite,
almost speak warmly to her,
almost give myself away for once.

The State of Nature

The woman and I approach the glass doors
exactly opposed, the distance between us
narrowing, as if the doors are a mirror
and she my image. As we enter the range
of the infrared detector the doors part
with a sharp intake and heave.
                                        She is fair
with an unhappy face and a clear blue eye.
This I see as our peripheral visions cross
like the gleams of swords, two strangers
barely aware – but aware! – of each other,
both slipping together for barely a second
into the state of nature. Too late

I see that she is only the new neighbour
whom I haven't met since the onset
of winter, and we must dally now and talk
for three or four minutes, grinning and flustered,
acting as if nothing had happened just now,
making embarrassment count as pleasant
surprise, repenting of our momentary fall.

The Hiding Place

I've been away so long, I'm sure
that something has happened here
after which there will never again
be a moment of all-out banter, except
during a moment of forgetfulness.
Someone whose mind has been elsewhere
will have turned around and seen us
and stopped smiling and decided
that the time has come to wake us
to our fair share of the real.
I open the door to find

the engines of the house
still ticking over at humdrum,
the weatherwoman talking far off
at low volume, the fireplace
chock-full of warm cliffs of ash,
my return as yet unmarked
except for a reader setting aside
a dishevelment of newspapers.

The Framing Shop

A wild-eyed horse's head, terraced rows
of schoolchildren in a buckling
newspaper photograph, a sun-hatted woman
ambling in all innocence through a field

of poppies, a prize-winner's certificate –
so many images from other worlds
that I prefer to stare dumbly ahead,
waiting my turn at the cluttered counter.

The frame maker's wife is nothing if not kind.
She marvels at whatever I bring in,
floating it on her fingertips before
laying it down lightly for the ceremony

of choosing mount and frame. This way,
she always brings out the best in me.
Today she places an L-shaped piece
of antique white against one side

of my picture, and on the opposite side
a rectangle of what she takes to be
pale ivory. I can see straight away
that they're the same, but I say: *The antique white*

is cooler and lighter, and sets off best
the warm tones of the gables and the winter
cherry trees. She nods and laughs, as much
as to say: *We know what we know, the two of us.*

We choose without delay a neutral wood
for the frame, and now, with pencil poised, she waits
for me to state my name – which I do, spelling out
carefully, as always, my surname.

The Rights of Man

How's your mum? I ask, as if I didn't know,
as if the sight of him had not brought to mind
the tumbling heights of fuchsia, the weave
of matted grass that was the lawn, the curtains
foxing in the sun. And he replies in kind,
his words as light as mine with civic intent.
He speaks (as he did the last time we met)
of her *little setback*, her need for the quiet life,
her fear of the knock at the door and the clatter
of the letter-box, her craving still for a cigarette –
her one comfort in life, he says, *that and the cup
of tea*. He smiles at the faint risquéness in his words,
not remembering that we've had all this before –
same words, same timing – because he's fighting
for his life, holding his own in the formal mode,
drawing a veil against the eye of a third party.
Any second now he'll cuff my shoulder, man
to man, and we must part once more as equals.

Three Recurring Dreams

Somewhere off a teeming main street,
the other side of canals and a plaza,
between churches and fruit barrows
there lurks the shop where I will find at last
Scot's *Discoverie of Witchcraft.*
Only there is never enough time.
Always the street turns around, all doors closed,
and I am striving back, lost! lost!
too late for the last train.

The bungalows are in the darkness, wooded over.
We are all back in the kitchen of the old house,
resurrected from the dung of a fallen roof.
Miraculous restorations! A fire again
on the blue-floored hearth,
the walls creamed with fresh, pale-green
distemper. A diffusion of warm and sacred light!
And beside the dresser, yellow well-water
glimmering in tinkers' cans.

The lake behind the houses has brimmed,
sheeting the fields with ice-bright water,
water up to the lowest branches,
water half-way up the white gables
of Ramolin. In the dark apple garden
the nettled earth parts and a body floats
into the rafters of the trees. Waking, drenched,
I am delirious with love of the world, the world
where a taxi turns and revellers go by, all talk.

Doorways

It was rare for all three doors across
        the middle of the old house
        to stand open at the same time
        because a draught would raise itself
        all at once and without warning
from nowhere to slam them shut in one go.
        But now and then when the laws
        of nature nodded on a halcyon day,
        you might leave all three flung wide
        and find that you could look for awhile
right through the house and see framed
        in the third doorway a back world
        of hen-run, dunghill and dock-leaf clump,
        far removed from the front world
        of pathway, clipped hedge and rose.

Table for One

In the sandy wind that scarpers in
off the prom, small skittering pieces
of litter (and in autumn dried leaves)
will go helter skelter under your feet
until you climb the steps to the entrance.
As you go inside, one world falls back

and away while another forms itself
slowly before your prickling eyes.
Here you will count for something,
even if there will be a price to pay.
You are called 'sir' as your coat is taken
with care and you are shown to the table

by the window, the only one with a view
of prom and sea and darkening sky,
all framed off now and picture-perfect.
Few enough words are spoken – 'yes,
the Caesar salad, the sea-bass, and oh yes,
a half bottle of the chardonnay' –

but these words are heard, taken down
and acted upon like no other words
you've spoken all week. The formal air,
the lowered voices, the low-key jazz
are what register here as most real
for now. And sometimes it can happen

that two or three women will come and sit
at the next table, and you can imagine
out of the corner of your eye that it is you
they are taking in when they pause from time
to time to glance in the direction of the sea,
even after the sea is well lost in the dark.

Convalescent, with Blue Deck Chair

Sitting with my back to the porch
in my all-too-collapsible deck chair
I gaze out towards the playing field
where two teams from the pub league
are playing a blinder across
the horizontal beams of August.

The calls of the players, the broken applause
from a small apostolate of onlookers,
the cries of the children down by the poplars –
all these come to me as born echoes
of themselves, beginning and ending distantly,
as if everything – life itself – were taking me easy.

The Good Host

This is the one in whose humbling
and slow-darkening house
you cannot help but rest.

This is the one who does not mind
what mills you've been through
of late, who lets the clock speak

louder than words,
lets the evening fall
beyond the need for words,

lets the stove
and the rain
and the wavering trees

fall together,

fall with you to sleep.

About the Author

Tom Duddy, originally from Shrule, Co. Mayo, has lived in Galway since the 1970s. He teaches Philosophy in the School of Humanities, National University of Ireland, Galway. His poems have been published in Irish and British magazines, and in several anthologies, including *Best of Irish Poetry 2007*, *Best of Irish Poetry 2010* and *The Forward Book of Poetry 2011*. HappenStance Press published his chapbook, *The Small Hours*, in 2006.

Acknowledgements

Thanks are due to the editors of the following publications where some of these poems, or versions of them, have appeared:

Crannóg, Envoi, Magma, Other Poetry, Poetry Ireland Review, Seam, Smiths Knoll, Southword, The Dark Horse, The Frogmore Papers, The Irish Times, The Rialto, and *The SHOp*.

Special thanks are due to Helena Nelson of HappenStance Press for permission to reprint a number of poems from the chapbook, *The Small Hours*.